New Trader, Rich Trader 2

Good Trades, Bad Trades

Steve Burns and

Janna Burns

Books by Steve Burns

New Trader, Rich Trader

Show Me Your Options

How I Made $2,000,000 In The Stock Market. Now Revised And Updated For The 21st Century

How I Made Money Using the Nicolas Darvas System

How to Get Followers on Twitter

Books by Janna Burns

New Trader, Rich Trader

New Trader, Rich Trader 2

Good Trades, Bad Trades

Lessons for Making Money in the Stock Market

CONTENTS

FOREWORD

I have had the great honor of knowing Steve Burns for several years now and so was thrilled to hear of the authoring of a sequel to his trading classic, "New Trader, Rich Trader". Throughout our friendship, Steve has consistently demonstrated the uncanny ability to analyze various problems and biases of the New Trader and articulate such issues in a unique and accessible manner.

As a result, when Steve and Janna asked me to write the Forward to, "New Trader, Rich Trader 2", I knew I was in for an entertaining and insightful journey. Their book did not disappoint. In contrast to its precursor, "New Trader, Rich Trader", where New Trader struggled with basic issues such as development of a positive expectancy method, position sizing as well as determining which assets to trade; in this manuscript all those issues have been resolved and so at the book's inception one might imagine New Trader would simply be relating his successes to Rich Trader.

As anyone who has successfully transitioned from "New Trader" to "Rich Trader" can attest, this is not the case and our authors brilliantly navigate New Trader's journey from knowing how to trade "in theory" towards flawless implementation of his positive expectancy model despite draw downs, missed opportunities, price shock events, and so on. As in all of Steve's books, I am consistently amazed at how despite his obvious mastery of our business he can recall with intimate detail what it was like to make the full gamut of "New Trader" mistakes.

"New Trader, Rich Trader 2" will have New Traders

reaching for their highlighters while Rich Traders smile knowingly at distance memories of painful missteps. Wherever you are in the journey from New to Rich Trader, this book is an indispensable tool filled with lots of "Aha" moments. To Steve and Janna, congratulations on a job well done, to all the New Traders reading this, pat yourself on the back for having found an indispensable aid in your journey from novice to pro.

Richard L. Weissman, Professional Trader and Author, *Trade Like a Casino*

"Trading is not the path to free money; profits must be earned through homework, discipline, courage, patience, and perseverance in the markets."

— Rich Trader

INTRODUCTION

There are many questions that a trader has to answer before entering a trade. There is a big difference between a good trade and a bad trade. The primary difference between good traders and bad traders is that good traders consistently make good trades, while bad traders make consistently bad trades. A good trade does not always make money and a bad trade is sometimes profitable. However, this does not change the definitions of right and wrong, good or bad. Trades should be measured by the quality of the reasoning for taking them. If traders consistently take trades that exercise their edge over the markets, they will make money in the long term. The worst thing that can happen for a new trader is being rewarded for a bad trade. This short-term win can result in long-term failure when his luck runs out and the market changes.

My purpose and goal in this book is to show the reader the difference between a good trade, one that is made inside the parameters of a trading plan with an edge, and a bad trade that is emotionally based on greed, fear, or opinion. In the long term, traders are a success or failure based on the quality of their trades.

The creation of bad trades is easy: trade your opinion, trade big, don't cut your losses, just hold on and hope. Bad trades fight trends; they put out a lot of money with the risk of making little. The entry and exit signals for bad trades are hope and fear, with the ego stepping in and refusing to honor the stop loss.

Good trades require work. The right trades come only after doing the required homework: chart studies, researching historical price action, or back testing along with research of chart patterns. In markets, price action can stay inside a range or they can trend. The job of the trader is to discover how to profit from these patterns over the long term. Trading price action is only the first part of a good trade; without risk management and discipline no trade is a good trade.

The purpose of this book is to take the reader through the principles and the differences between good trades and bad trades.

PART I

MANAGING THE MIND TO STAY IN THE GAME

"Dramatic and emotional trading experiences tend to be negative; pride is a great banana peel, as are hope, fear, and greed. My biggest slipups occurred shortly after I got emotionally involved with positions."

— *Ed Seykota*

CHAPTER 1

A good trade is taken with complete confidence and follows your trading method; a bad trade is taken on an opinion.

"It's not the mathematical skill that's critical to winning; it's the discipline of being able to stick to the system."

— Blair Hull

New Trader walked through the rain to Rich Trader's front door. He knocked twice. When Rich Trader arrived at the door, what a sight New Trader was: drenched and dripping wet from head to toe.

"Can you not afford an umbrella?" Rich Trader asked.

"I can, it is the planning to keep one with me that I fall short on," he answered.

"Well, come in out of the rain. It has been awhile," Rich Trader motioned him inside.

After New Trader took off his wet coat and shoes and got settled in a comfortable chair, he sat drinking hot tea by the fireplace, pondering the past year. Rich Trader appeared as comfortable as ever in loafers, a polo shirt, and slacks.

"What brings you to my humble abode today? It has been quite a while," he asked.

"Well, I did not want to be a nuisance after you so generously gave me so much of your time last year. You taught me all the fundamental principles for successful trading and I felt it was up to me to go use them," New Trader said appreciatively.

"So how did you do?" he asked.

"I finished up 22% last year in my trading account," New Trader answered proudly.

Rich Trader gave him a look of disappointment. "I didn't ask about your returns, I asked how YOU did. One year's return has very little to do with you; that can be pure random chance. My concern is you, your discipline, your focus, your risk management, your stress management, your system-building and system-following skills. So how did you do?" Rich Trader asked again.

"It was a learning experience. With real money on the line I discovered things about myself that I thought I had moved past. I once again experienced fear of losing, greed of wanting to trade too big, my ego wanting to be right. I found myself trading more against my own negative emotional states than the market's price movements, "New Trader explained.

"That is a normal experience with new traders moving from the classroom to the arena. You want to prove something to yourself and to others. A trader's goal is to be above those impulses which lead you to making wrong decisions. Instead, most traders allow their fear, greed, and ego to send their money to the accounts of the disciplined traders who simply follow the price action," said Rich Trader.

"Isn't that the truth! The more I traded, the more I realized trading is a mental game, not a numbers game. I found myself making up excuses to override my rules, only to discover that this interference only hurt my performance in the long term," he responded.

"The best trader you will ever be is that person who does research and development outside market hours. The worst trader you will ever be is someone who sits on a string of losses in a drawdown and wants to get back to even. While the market is closed, you as the trading analyst and researcher must decide what you the trader will do when the market is open. Your entries, exits, and position sizing should be determined by your mind when the markets are closed, not by your fear, greed, and ego while the market is open," Rich Trader said.

"My mistakes have been in my management of my own mind; that is where my trouble started. Trading is just not as fun as I had imagined it would be. Profits can be taken back after they are made so there is not really much to celebrate during winning trades. The losses were out of my control. The market goes where it wants. All I can do is to respect my stops and choose the size of my losses," New Trader responded.

"Exactly, and you are not your trading; you are the trader. You are simply following your plan. Trading is one of the few professions where even most successful practitioners have low winning percentages. Most professions, like being a doctor, a lawyer, engineer, or the like, demand huge winning percentages. For a doctor to fail in surgery is a catastrophe. The best lawyers win a large percentage of their cases. Traders are different. Some of the best trend-following traders have low win percentages like 30% or less, but still make money based on their huge wins being greater than all their losses. Oddly enough there are options sellers with 90% win rates who end up losing money in the long run because one loss in ten is bigger than the other nine wins; worse, the options seller blows up with one huge loss due to over leverage and the unexpected move that happens when they have no hedge in place. They high winning percentage traders are the rare ones and even they must keep their few losses small to stay profitable. Most traders have 50% or less winning percentages and their profitability emerges from their wins simply being bigger than their losses.

Most traders are more like batters in baseball than any other profession. Regardless of how good a batter is, hitting and getting on base is only accomplished one-third of the time. Batters have to follow their process of when to swing and when to not swing for the greatest odds of getting a hit. Two strike outs in a game are quickly forgiven if the third at-bat results in a grand slam homerun. The best professional baseball players do not have a self-esteem crisis after a strikeout or a few in a row; they know who they are and how they got to the big leagues and move on to the next at-bat. The success of a trading career and of a baseball career is based on the long-term process of sticking with what works," Rich Trader explained.

New Trader replied: "That is the hard part, sticking with the process when you lose over and over again. It is when doubt about myself and my system creeps in."

"The fuel that takes a new trader from wanting to be a successful trader to being a success is desire, passion, faith, resources, and knowledge. If one of these elements is missing, the new trader may not make it over the bridge to get the prize. Desire knows what you want. The odds of you getting what you want start increasing once you have a target. Desire is the fuel that gives you the energy to do the work required to be a successful trader.

Passion gives you the energy to research, do back tests, and not stop until you find the system that works for you. Passion is the fuel of perseverance. With enough perseverance, the only thing that separates you from your goals is time.

Faith knows the outcome before you begin. You know who you will become and you are willing to do the work to get there. Faith is a very powerful force. Many times your life will line up the way you believe it will; through the power of your actions, your subconscious starts taking you where you want to be.

Traders have to have the resources to make the journey to success. You have to build yourself enough capital to get in the game. You need access to the right mentors and like-minded traders for support. You have to have the mental resources to deal with failure to get through to success. You need to build up your knowledge through study — the study of successful traders, the study of charts, price action, and risk management. Mentors can help you build the foundational knowledge of what works with trading the markets. Mentors can only teach you and show you and tell you how to swim. You have to swim over the river yourself.

So why are you having trouble consistently swimming over the river using the right form?" Rich Trader asked.

New Trader answered after three minutes of staring at Rich Trader with a puzzled look.

"Fear of drowning, fear of waves, fear of whether or not

I am a good swimmer."

"So does your problem with trading a system consistently lie within your own mind or with the quality of your chosen trading method?" he asked.

New Trader paused again, and then answered.

"I am the problem, or better yet, my lack of controlling my thoughts and emotions is the root of all my problems."

"The trader is the weakest link in any trading system. The trader, more than even the system he is trading, is the ultimate determiner of success or failure. Once a robust system has been chosen, it is the ability to take entries and exits consistently with discipline while managing risk which makes a skilled trader. This is what leads to trading success. This is the Holy Grail so many traders seek, yet so many can't even understand," Rich Trader concluded.

New Trader sat back in his chair listening to the fire crackling in the fireplace with an empty cup of tea in hand, pondering why Rich Trader's explanation sounded so easy yet was so hard to do with real money on the line.

CHAPTER 2

A good trade is taken with a disciplined entry and position size; a bad trade is taken to win back losses the market owes you.

"Ninety-five percent of the trading errors you are likely to make — causing the money to just evaporate before your eyes — will stem from your attitudes about being wrong, losing money, missing out, and leaving money on the table."

—- Mark Douglas

"I will be right back," New Trader said, getting up from the company meeting he was attending.

One of the other managers sent him a knowing frown as he left, but he really didn't care. The market was dropping, and it was all he could think about.

So, for the third time in as many hours, he pulled out his phone — which he normally loved but hated the app's tiny stupid buttons — and looked up his stock.

It had dropped another point, and his stomach dropped.

Pull out. His mind was screaming, *don't lose any more money! Forget the signal, just get out now!*

He gulped, his palms feeling sweaty... his plan said to wait for the signal, but it had been going down all day and it was almost at the stopping point.

He pressed the buttons, feeling a migraine coming on. It was too late now, though, and he had lost about $1,300.

Well, that and the commissions.

When he left that day checking his phone, he could have smacked himself. In fact, he almost did. If he had followed his plan, he'd have been up almost $1,000 and still rising.

Stupid, stupid, stupid! Follow the plan, not your fear!

He scowled as he drove to the little cafe he and Rich Trader usually met at. Once he got there, he found his mentor and greeted him with a tight smile.

"Thanks for coming to meet me."

"Well, of course. I *do* rather enjoy eating here, they have the *best* coffee."

New Trader smiled at him, lest strained this time.

"What's troubling you?" the older man asked, sipping his coffee as his eyes searched for the waitress.

"Oh, it's nothing, I just..." he began with a sigh. "I did it again. I let my fear take over and I lost a *lot* of money; but if I had followed my system and waited for the signal, I could have *made* money!"

Rich Trader shook his head. "But that's not the most important part. It's not about the actual money gained or lost; it's about *discipline* and controlling emotional impulses. Though this is also a prime example of *why* you should follow your system."

"Yeah, I know..." New Trader said with a sigh, stirring the coffee Rich Trader had already been considerate enough to order him. "But now it's just... how did you deal with losses?"

"Well, first I had to learn the hard way that I didn't know better than the market," Rich Trader began with a chuckle.

"I would sit here at this very cafe and watch the market rise or fall, thinking I knew it all, that I could predict the market better than my plan that I had spent hours upon hours making. Other times the market would scream at me to go short as I continued to buy support levels even as they broke one after another. Then it was all hope, not thought. My predictions and my pride replaced the reality of what was taking place."

He paused to take a sip of coffee. "And then you also have to consider what a loss actually *is*. For me, a loss is not when I lose money; it's when *I don't follow my plan.*"

New Trader smiled guiltily.

"So in that respect, it is very rare that I lose anymore. I might lose money, but I don't lose confidence. Ah, thank you, Jane."

Their usual waitress smiled at him as she gave them both their usual: the Tuesday special, minus the sauce.

"No prob, boys," she said, winking at New Trader playfully as she left.

"She's a rather nice girl," Rich Trader commented and his younger companion scowled.

"I *have* a girlfriend, thanks. Anyways, it doesn't matter. How do I deal with these strings of losses?" New Trader asked, taking a bite. "Well, *unprofitable trades,* I suppose I should say."

"Well, I would begin with shrinking your position sizes. This means that as you lose money you lose less and are at your smallest position sizing, as well as minimizing your exposure during losing streaks. Then you would start to grow your position size again as you start to win. The way

PRICE / 200 DMA

I trade in volatile, choppy, and range-bound markets is to risk very little or stay fully in cash. I wait for a breakout or trend to emerge. I will also buy into reversals at key levels that have a high probability edge. I'm in no hurry to rush into anything. I'll still eat if I trade. There's no reason to rush into more losses. Much of our trading comes down to a battle between our patience and our impulses."

"That... makes sense," New Trader said, pondering his words as he stared at his food. "It makes *perfect* sense, actually. I hadn't thought of that as an angle for position sizing. Most people new to trading increase position size to get back to even during draw downs but end up hurting themselves in every way – financially, mentally, and emotionally. It makes sense to turn down the heat when you're getting smoked."

Rich Trader chuckled, mildly impressed. "That is an excellent analogy there, for sure."

New Trader continued, encouraged by his mentor's praise. "So it's really just my passion fanning the flames and making me wound up and tense... how should I cool myself off?"

"Passions have to be channeled into what will help you the most: research, development, and further educating yourself. Live trading is where strong passions and desires are *least* needed. Improperly used, passion and desire will make you want to push for more and take bigger risks. The calm, rational trader is the best trader. He won't press and want things to happen; this is *dangerous*. We cannot *will* the market to do what we want, we can only watch and wait. So save your intensity and use it *outside* market hours, where your real money isn't at risk."

New Trader nodded. "Right, it's all about getting centered and following the process. Not trying to hit the ball out of the park every swing. It's about form and composure and taking the right swings at the plate."

Rich Trader chuckled. "You remembered that?"

"Of course," New Trader said. "I remember everything you teach me... I just don't always learn it the easy way."

"Fair enough," Rich Trader said with a fond smile. "Well, when a trader has the right process down, their wins and losses are defined by their ability to follow that system. That's when the breakthrough occurs. A trader isn't their results or their P&L; they're just the witness of what's happening to their system. Losses should inspire *curiosity*, not a crisis of faith. And once you've accomplished that feat, a trader will cross the road from the majority to the minority with a mental edge over the other participants."

New Trader finished his meal, resting his napkin over his plate.

"Trading isn't just about short term profitability ..." he murmured thoughtfully. "Profits come from traders' consistency in trading the markets they're in, whether that's daily, weekly, monthly, or over the course of their lives."

"Exactly," Rich Trader said, back to sipping his tea. "Trend followers do great in trends, option sellers make money when the strike price isn't reached in their short option, and reversion-to-the-mean traders do well inside range bound markets. It's not the trader, it's the system. Our job as traders is to build those systems and trade with a methodology that we can follow consistently through different market environments."

"When the stars align we have to be there to collect our bucket of money," Rich Trader said with a smile that bordered on a smirk. "Trading is not about outcomes; it's about the process. Outcomes can be random but the process must be robust. A good trading process will lead to capital appreciation over the long term as long as the trader can follow that process and not drift from it in unfavorable market environments."

"So basically, a good trader is one who finds the robust system, then trades it with discipline and focus? And that's the game? Profits and losses are completely out of our hands?"

"Of course not... Traders choose the size of their losses when they honor their original stops. Traders also choose to have bigger wins if they allow a winning trade to run and let a trailing stop decide when the run is over – rather than deciding based on a target, opinion, or fear of losing profits. And all these choices should be made ahead of time, inside a trailing plan and outside market hours."

"So the trading plan is my boss?" New Trader said blandly.

"Well, I suppose in a way. But it's a boss that you have full control over, whereas your emotions and ego is a boss you would be hard-pressed to restrain."

"So I am a planner first and foremost?" New Trader asked as the bill arrived and their plates were taken away.

"Well, it's the first piece of the puzzle perhaps. What will most determine your trading success is your ability to build a robust system based on a method with an edge. Then you formulate a trading plan which follows that system in a way that can be profitable in the long term. The hardest part is actually *following* your plan and letting it play out without fear or pride getting in the way. "

"Right," New Trader said, leaving his usual tip on the table. "That sums it all up rather nicely. I'll get right to it."

Rich Trader laughed, shaking his head.

He remembered those days.

CHAPTER 3

A good trade is taken when your entry parameters line up; a bad trade is taken out of fear of missing a move.

"Essentially, what you fear is not the markets but rather your inability to do what you need to do, when you need to do it, without hesitation."

– Mark Douglas

"So it's really about the *mindset,* not your predictions. Like when I..." He could see it happening. Her eyes stared to glaze, her head tilted, and when he was done she would say...

"That's great, honey. It's so good that you're making all that money on the stock market."

He gave her a dull look. That wasn't even what he said. But most people seemed to go off into their own world once he started talking about trading, so it really wasn't that surprising.

"Right."

"Maybe one day you can quit and do it full time!"

"Yeah, that would be nice. I'd get to wear my pajamas to work!" he said with a laugh, though the look on her face said she wasn't fond of the idea.

"You'd make *so* much more money doing that anyways. Why don't you just do it?" she said – a discussion they'd had many times.

"Because I still want a steady income to supplement my losses; I'm not comfortable doing that yet."

She rolled her eyes. "Buy low, sell high... it can't be *that* hard."

For a moment, he had no reply to her comment.

"Then why don't *you* do it?"

"I don't have enough money to start an account, and it all looks so complicated. But you understand all those charts and things, so you should make money like crazy! Isn't that what you're always saying?"

"It is *so* much more complicated than that! Were you listening *at all* to what I was just saying? It takes *discipline* and... You know what? Let's just drop this. There's no reason to argue and I'm about to run late for my lunch with Rich Trader."

"Oh, I see."

"What?"

"You're going to see 'Rich Trader,' right?"

"Yes."

She rolled her eyes. "*Whatever.*"

He gave her an incredulous look before leaving for his usual cafe.

Women.

When he arrived, Rich Trader was laughing at something Jane had said. She looked up as New Trader entered, smiling at him.

"The usual?"

He nodded, his smile back strained.

She left, his coffee already on the table with two packets of sweetener.

"So, how are you on this beautiful afternoon?" Rich Trader asked, stirring his tea.

"Fine. Just trying to figure everything out."

"You mean with your trading mentality?"

New Trader nodded.

"Well, what were your biggest errors last year?"

"Well... I wasn't patient. I wouldn't wait for the right entries or I'd start chasing after some trades. Sometimes it worked out, but not usually."

Rich Trader laughed. "Good trades are like buses. If you miss one, you just wait for the next one to arrive. The world is full of buses and just as full of good setups for trading. As a trade breaks out at your buy signal, the further the move away from its key level and the more risks there are in chasing it."

"Yeah, and if you miss the entry you might also miss the bulk of the move," New Trader said, thanking the waitress when she brought his food.

"Even when a trend really runs it will usually give you another shot at entry as it pulls back to the nearest support on the way to going back up. **In the long run, patience pays better than boldness for traders,**" Rich Trader said. "The ability to consistently trade only the highest probability entry setups will be one of the determinants of a trader's long-term success in the markets. Continuously chasing moves that are already out of the gate is a sure way to grind your account down with losses."

Rich Trader took a moment to sip his coffee before continuing.

"The reason the vast majority of new traders never make it is that they take entry signals based on their emotions. They're afraid to miss a move so they chase after a stock after it's already broken out and run. It becomes too tempting after they've watched it day in and day out, so they just can't take it anymore and buy. And this low probability trade is, many times, right at the time other traders who entered at the right price level are taking their profits and exiting. So the move is over or the price is going back to base."

New Trader nodded. "Or going short when you should be going long."

Rich Trader nodded. "Yes. The wrong time to short is usually when a stock is finally breaking out of a price base into all-time new highs and the new trader thinks it's time to go short. What the new trader doesn't understand is that the stock is going from range-bound to trending and they are shorting when they should be going long. The breakout signals that sellers in the old price range have been overcome by buyers wanting in, and the stock is under accumulation so it's searching for a new price range and will trend until it finds one. Usually, a short at all-time highs is ego-based because the new trader wants to be the one who can say that they shorted at the highs."

New Trader nodded, finishing his mouthful of food before replying.

"It's strange how my emotions flood to the surface when

it's time to take entries and exits. Fear, greed, ego... they all want me to stray from my written trading plan."

"Yes, but your trading plan is written to make money in the long term, while your emotions are trying to protect you from losses in the short term. Your fear is trying to protect your profit from turning into a loss, while your trading plan wants a small profit to turn into a big profit. Your greed wants to chase a trade that has already happened while your trading plan wants to enter a trade before it has the big moves. Your ego wants to be right about a trade in the short term, while your trading plan wants to make money in the long term."

"So, basically, as usual, my biggest battle is trading my actual plan, not my emotions."

Rich Trader chuckled. "Yes... very frustrating, isn't it? Finding an edge over price movements is a job in and of itself; don't compound the difficulty of trading with an edge by having to battle your emotions. Coming up with a trading plan is not the hardest part of trading; once you get this far, following it with perseverance, discipline, and risk management is what separates winning traders from losing traders."

"So after you've gone through all the trouble of doing research and development and built your trading plan, then you have to actually follow what it's telling you. The researcher and scientist in you did all the work; now it is up to the trader within to do what it's being told to do."

Rich trader nodded. "You have to root out all the reasons why you broke your trading plan. Look inside yourself and ask: Why? What caused me to panic, sell, chase, risk too much, try too hard, and generally do what most losing traders do? You have to answer these questions if you are to be successful."

They paused to eat their food. Minutes later, Rich Trader broke the silence.

"Do you know the single primary determiner of trading success?"

"...Self control?"

"Yes. Your success will be based on your ability to control yourself in your trading."

New Trader paused in thought.

"If I'm not in control, then my emotions are: my impulses, bad attitude, preconceived beliefs about how things work, the fight or flight instinct, maybe even a self-constructed ego that feels threatened by failure or even by success."

Rich Trader nodded. "You're none of these things; don't let them take you over."

"Yet... if none of these things are me, then what exactly am I?"

"You are the witness of all these things. If you change perspective and see these things for what they are, you are not them; you are human consciousness witnessing what arises in your field of consciousness. You can let them take over or you can see them for what they are and make decisions based on your mind and your will. You can make decisions that take you where you want to go in life or you can let external elements influence you and take you where you don't want to go. It's a choice of staying in control or allowing yourself to be swept away by waves of external factors which warp your decision-making process."

So following a trading plan is to simply trade it in the present moment without any other meanings attached to it? It's just one trade of many?"

"Exactly, to follow a trading plan you have to disconnect any one trade's meaning from anything other than what it actually is. It is not a battle for self-worth. It is not the determinant of your financial future. One trade should not have any impact on your emotions or life; it's just one trade of the next 100 if you're doing it right. If it has more meaning than just one trade of the next one hundred, then you are trading too big. Your system's draw downs are too big, you have too much risk at one time, or you are trading for a living when you should be building your capital and paying off bills."

"So trading should just be trading. There should be no internal story, no external meaning beyond the P&L?"

Rich Trader nodded.

"Yes. If there's more to your trading than just trading, you're doing something wrong. Find out what it is, correct it, and then move on."

CHAPTER 4

A good trade is taken to be profitable in the context of your trading plan; a bad trade is taken out of greed to make a lot of money quickly.

"Experienced traders control risk, inexperienced traders chase gains."

— Alan Farley

"What happened *now?*"

New Trader looked at his girlfriend with a newfound sense of annoyance.

"I lost money," he said. *Best to keep it simple.*

"*Again?*" she asked with a frown.

"I *told* you it would take time to learn. And no one wins *every* time!"

"Well, maybe you shouldn't be doing it then! It's just gambling away your money."

He groaned, rubbing his temples. "No, it's... I really don't want to have this conversation again."

She narrowed her eyes at him. "*Fine.* Don't listen to me and just gamble all your hard-earned money away!" she exclaimed before storming off.

He rubbed his eyes. Sometimes she just made him so *tired.* It's like the more he tried, the worse everything got.

Sort of like my trades recently, he thought with an inner

laugh. He and Rich Trader had talked about it recently.

"Greedy trading is bad trading," Rich Trader had told him. *"You want to always be trading the probabilities, not what you want to happen. The worse entry signal that any trader can take is based on their greed. The worse exit signal is based on fear. Entries and exits have to be built around the probability of winning, no on what profits you want to make."*

It was strange, because he remembered Jane standing in front of the table for a good while before collecting their plates.

"You can work as hard as you want in research to develop a trading system and a plan that works for you. However, you then have to follow that plan. Athletes can train and practice all they want, but when they enter the real game they have to follow the rules or they won't win. Breaking your own trading game rules defeats you."

He thought about it some more.

"Trading in more like a sport of finesse than a sport of effort. Golfers win because of the right technique and method, not by trying harder. If you are a bad golfer, practice and effort mean nothing in a game. You are simply reinforcing bad habits and wasting time and energy. The real point of golfing and trading is to have the right technique, then use it with discipline and mental toughness over and over again. Success comes from using winning principles with perseverance and discipline over a long period of time until they pay off in a big way. "

He remembered reiterating the fact that work, effort, and homework were for when the market was closed;

discipline and self-control were for when the market was open.

"A trader is like a surfer who cannot control the size of the waves. All he can do is to ride the waves the best he can. He can study the times of day and weather conditions that create different-sized waves to get an edge on what to expect, but all he can do after all the practice and study is ride the waves."

His own wanting to make money had led him to make the mistakes of trading too big and risking too much, putting effort where there should have been patience and trading when he should have waited.

Once again, he was the weakest link in his own trading system. He seemed to have two trading impulses: the Analyst and the Greedy Trader. The Analyst went through the charts and back tested calmly, seeing what worked over long periods of time. The Analyst was calm and self-controlled. He enjoyed trading and looked forward to when the markets opened.

Then there was Greedy Trader who wanted to make money at all costs. He believed he was much cleverer than the other traders, though there was little evidence of this. Greedy Trader believed he could override Analyst's trading plan and do whatever he liked.

Greedy Trader liked to trade big, with false confidence in his skills as a discretionary trader. He proved to be a fool in most circumstances but continued to try to make big profits.

New Trader had to kill the egoism that gave life to this aggressive, internal Greedy Trader before it killed his account – sort of like his girlfriend who sometimes tried to kill his checking account.

He sighed. He wanted to be a successful and profitable trader *so badly.*

So he knew what he needed to do. He needed to focus on self-control and process and let the results fall where they may. He needed to give up control of results and focus on his role in the process.

His true focus had to be to manage risk, follow his method, and stay mentally disciplined, letting the results fall where they may. If he wanted to rework his system or trading plan, that had to be done in the off-market hours and planned before the trading day began.

Of course, as Rich Trader told him, his desire to make money was misplaced. He should desire to be a great trader who follows process.

After all, trading profits are the outcome of following a robust process, not trying to make sudden decisions with no context. Your mind must be that of an entrepreneur running a business, not the mind of a gambler at the roulette wheel.

Traders get themselves in trouble when they stray from the risk/reward probabilities of a situation and trade according to their self-delusions of being a special trader who can outsmart the markets. Eventually and inevitably, that will end badly.

"I am a businessman, not a gambler," he said quietly before getting up to work on his system.

CHAPTER 5

A good trade is taken according to your trading plan; a bad trade is taken to inflate the ego.

"The most important change in my trading career occurred when I learned to divorce my ego from the trade. Trading is a psychological game. Most people think that they're playing against the market, but the market doesn't care. You're really playing against yourself. You have to stop trying to will things to happen in order to prove that you're right. Listen only to what the market is telling you now. Forget what you thought it was telling you five minutes ago. The sole objective of trading is not to prove you're right, but to hear the cash register ring."

— Martin Schwartz

"Do you know what a trader's biggest obstacle to success is?" Rich Trader asked, stirring his sweetener into his coffee as he watched the sun disappear into the sea. The days always seemed to end so early now.

What answer was he looking for? Risk management, trading with the trend, not fighting the market? It could be so many things...

"Fighting the actual price action?"

"Close," Rich Trader said with a smile, sipping his coffee."Not managing the risk of ruin?' New Trader tried again.

"Why would you fight price action or trade so big that you could blow up your account?" the older man asked genuinely, brow raised.

"Because I really want to make a lot of money and I don't want to admit when I'm wrong."

"And what causes you to want to make a lot of money and hold on to a losing position?"

"I want to prove I'm a great trader to myself and to my family and friends?"

"Is that a question or an answer? And if it's a question, why?"

"I suppose because I'm not yet sure myself."

"These are all things that you must know before putting real money at risk. Trading in the markets is a very expensive place to 'find yourself.' Counseling is much cheaper than trading. Fear, greed, and ego are very expensive monkeys to have on your back while trading. They spend all day telling you to let losing trades run, cut winners short, and forget your trading plan to prove you are right. Your biggest competitor in the markets is not other traders but yourself. You determine your entry and exit plan, no one else."

"So my trading success is all about my own self-control?" New Trader asked.

"If you listen to nothing else I say, hear this: You have the proper sequence of events reversed. First, realize you are a trader. That is who you are and what you decide to be. Then your identity is not based on trading results; it is based on who you are. You have nothing to prove to yourself or to anyone else. There is a big difference between knowing who and what you are and hoping to become it in the future. An acorn will become an oak, regardless of any other opinions. The potential is always there. With the potential inside, all that's left is for the acorn to grow and become what it was meant to be. An acorn simply grows, unleashing what is inside with no self-doubt or reinforcement from other acorns.

If a crop fails, a farmer is still a farmer. He doesn't have to question his own identity based on results. A farmer's self-worth is not shaken by a bad drought or storm because he has decided to be a farmer. While there may be pain of loss and financial battles, he still knows who he is through both success and failure."

Rich Trader paused, looking over the landscape before settling deeper into his lounge chair.

"If you truly want to be a trader, you must know who you are and where you want to go. Once you believe in your own identity and know what your goals are; only time separates you from your destination. Once you are free from internal conflict and self-doubt, you have energy to do the work required to take you where you want to go. Trading is a difficult game to learn and be successful at continually. Traders do not have the luxury of being double-minded about themselves. Either we are or we are not traders. Every day we have to make that choice and get to work. Our self-worth and identity cannot fluctuate with our account capital."

"How I see myself and my internal identity is a source of so much of my stress and inner conflict. I can certainly see how that can lead to anxiety."

"The traders who really make it in this business started

out trapped in a new trader's body with a new trader's account to work with. You will notice that didn't stop them from realizing their potential. The key was that they made a decision based on their conviction that trading is what they would be doing. Most had no Plan 'B' or had a strong motivation never to have to use it. They made their decision of what they were before any results confirmed that they would succeed. The big secret is that once they decided on their path, the only thing that separated them from their goals was time. If they got up every morning and made decisions that kept them going in the direction of their passions and dreams, they were literally unstoppable from the outside; only they could stop their own momentum from the inside. It is very hard to beat the trader who never stops learning, never stops growing, and never gives up."

"So being mentally locked into a long-term goal could really ease much of the stress," New Trader said thoughtfully.

"Yes, a new trader must understand that a trade is just a trade; he has to know he is playing for the big picture – his trading career. And *that* is a long process that should dilute much of the daily stress. One day should be just $1/365^{th}$ of a year of trading, and one trade should just be one of the next 100 trades. The ego should not even show up on the charts. The charts should be traded for what they are, and the trader's emotions and ego should never become entangled with price action."

"Keeping that principle in mind, it's like having a volume dial on your emotions. Putting any one trade into that kind of perspective makes it lose the egotistic and emotional interference."

"Exactly," said Rich Trader. "Trading success comes from first researching what the right decisions are to be profitable and then being able to stick to those right decisions when the time comes and not be stopped by internal barriers."

New Trader nodded; then his phone buzzed.

When are you coming home?

He frowned.

"The misses?" Rich Trader asked.

"Yeah, I guess I should head home. As always, thank you for your wonderful advice and coffee."

"Any time," Rich Trader said as he watched his pupil leave with slumped shoulders.

CHAPTER 6

A good trade is taken without regret or internal conflict; a bad trade is taken when a trader is double-minded.

"A double minded man is unstable in all his ways."

— James 1:8 KJV Bible

It was a beautiful afternoon, the sky bright and clear. The birds were singing and New Trader was enjoying his weekly meal with Rich Trader.

"Most traders make the mistake of focusing on a trading method when they first start out, when they really need to focus on themselves," Rich Trader began as their food was taken away and their usual waitress filled their drinks. "The dividing line between winners and losers in the markets is not their trading method; it's their self-control and ability to manage risk. The trader can't control the profitable outcome of a trade, only the downside stop if they're wrong – and *all* traders would do well to focus on the area under their control. This is good news because the success and failure of any trading method is determined by risk management and position sizing more than anything else."

"I see," New Trader said as his phone buzzed.

His girlfriend was calling him again.

He sent it to voicemail before they continued their conversation.

"There are many robust systems that can be found with diligent research through back testing historical price data, but a system in and of itself is not as important as the trader trading it. Boredom, impatience, fear, and greed are typically a trader's undoing, not their method," Rich Trader said. "Most new traders get to step one, having a method, and think they're done, when really that's when the work begins: trading that method with discipline, consistency, and self-control over and over again without quitting when they meet resistance and failure."

New Trader nodded, waiting for the inevitable analogy.

"That's where the rubber meets the road. Not in some fancy delusion of finding the magic Holy Grail to profitable trading. If someone ever did find free money they would quickly become wealthy beyond imagination until they were unable to scale it any higher due to trading size. I'm *fairly* certain that the Holy Grail trader would not be selling it for $19.99 online. The day a trader quits looking for a magic recipe and just trades the best system available, that's the day he grows up."

"So it seems the biggest problem I've had in the past year is that I stopped focusing on my method and put it on myself instead. It was all about me and how my self-esteem was connected to my results. I became my trading; my wins made me a winner and my losses made me a loser. I got too emotionally wrapped up in the money and lost my perspective."

"Yes, that's it exactly. Traders can't mix their emotional capital with their financial capital. Those accounts need to be separate. Your wins and losses shouldn't be making deposits or withdrawals from your emotional accounts. Those currencies should *never* be exchanged. They should be maintained far apart from each other."

"And how should I do that?"

"Just like one trade is only one of the next 100, your trading should only be a small percentage of your life. If your entire self-worth is tied up in being a successful trader, it will greatly amplify every win and loss. Every weekly, monthly, and annual P&L will have a greater impact on you emotionally and mentally," Rich Trader said. "If your life is diversified, if you're a spouse in a good marriage, a parent, enjoy time with friends, have hobbies, enjoy social settings, entertainment, take care of your health through diet and nutrition, and continue to learn and improve yourself, then trading results will have far less impact. The beauty of trading is that for most traders there is forced downtime, when the markets close or in market environments that are not conducive to the trader's methodology. We have to take some time off from active trading. And if you're trend trading and just riding a wave, you have plenty of time to go enjoy life and then check in at the close."

"Well, that is another problem I had: Too much unnecessary screen time and too much obsessing over results 24/7. So basically you're prescribing me a 'chill pill'?"

"I'm saying always do what you should be doing, and part of that process involves doing nothing at times and balancing your life to avoid burnout or damage to your mental health. The same work ethic and drive that can make us successful can also hurt us if we don't stay focused on why we are trading in the first place. The real reason we trade is to pursue happiness, whatever that looks like for us. Some enjoy the game itself while others do it for freedom or as a lifestyle choice. The thing is, we're going in the wrong direction if we become unhappy as a result of trading. We are not trading for the pursuit of *un*happiness; when that dark cloud comes, it is time to stop and reevaluate what we're doing wrong and why we are on the wrong path."

"I suppose the parameters of risk/reward and maximum equity draw downs play a huge part in this pursuit of happiness."

"A robust trading method does a trader no good if they can't mentally and emotionally deal with the stress of trading it," Rich Trader said with a quiet laugh. "You have to trade within your own comfort zone and only add position sizing and more risk as your strength to handle your stress is no longer an issue. Trading is a process of growth, not quantum leaps. Nothing good comes from trading above the level you are comfortable with."

"So what else do you prescribe for strengthening the weakest part of the trading system, otherwise known as 'me'?"

"Each trader has to find a personal philosophy that's bigger than they are to ground them and give them internal strength and faith. Some traders understand their place in the greater universe and that gives them perspective on the size of their problems. Others seek a spiritual path that leads to increasing levels of enlightenment about who they are. Many traders practice daily meditation to understand how to bring the internal chatter of thoughts and emotions under control, or they find power in practicing mindfulness throughout the day. Some traders find comfort in prayer and faith in a higher power. These practices bring perspective to how big of a deal trading really is in the greater schemes of things and may make it easier to take your entries and exits."

New Trader nodded. "I see. I'll think about this."

"Of course," Rich Trader said, relaxing in his seat, evidently in no rush to leave as their checks were delivered by a smiling Jane.

New Trader's phone buzzed again, and this time when he looked down his expression quickly shifted to one of surprise, then confusion, before going blank.

It's over. I'm done. Seriously.

For a moment it felt crushing, devastating.

But then he felt a huge weight lifted off his shoulders. He shouldn't feel this way about his girlfriend of three years. But really, this had been a long time coming.

PART II

CREATING A ROBUST METHODOLOGY

"In order of importance to me are: 1) the long-term trend, 2) the current chart pattern, and 3) picking a good spot to buy or sell."

— Ed Seykota

CHAPTER 7

A good trade is based on your trading plan; a bad trade is based on emotions and beliefs.

"To anticipate the market is to gamble. To be patient and react only when the market gives the signal is to speculate."
— Jesse Livermore

New Trader was out at the coffee shop feeling strangely... at peace. His girlfriend had moved out and he could focus on his trading.

But something still felt out of place...

"Well, hello there, stranger."

He looked up to see a pretty girl in a blue dress.

Her brow rose. "Don't recognize me? I'm Jane... from the cafe?"

"Oh! Right, Jane, the waitress!"

She rolled her eyes, taking a seat beside him. "*Yes*, Jane *the waitress...*"

He chuckled nervously, feeling uncomfortable. It's not like they had ever shared any real conversation.

"So how's your trading been going?"

"...What?" he asked after a slight pause.

"*How's your trading been going?*" she repeated. "I hear you and Rich Trader going on about it all the time."

"Well..." he replied slowly, trying to make sure he had

it figured out before he spouted off like he sometimes did for Rich Trader. "I think I've improved, but I'm still my own worst enemy."

"What do you mean?"

"I think I get in my own way," he said with a laugh, expecting the conversation to quickly degrade or become awkward. To his surprise, she continued with a thoughtful expression.

"You know what Rich Trader told me once? The wisdom is in the price action, not our opinions. Our skills in trading are based on how well we're able to hear what the charts are telling us and trade accordingly. It's when we start to predict what's going to happen instead of reacting to what *actually* happens that things start to go bad for our equity curve."

"Yeah..." New Trader agreed. "Our opinions and biases are based on illusions, not actual price action. And our job is to trade the price action that unfolds, not our opinions, predictions, or egos, which get in the way of our ability to make money."

She laughed. "Yeah, we're traders, not fortune tellers."

"We're traders?" New Trader thought to himself. He liked the sound of that.

"We have to... let's see, how would Rich Trader put it? Surfing the waves is good, but flowing like the waves is best. The most money is made by following where the market takes you, not guessing or hoping or believing or fighting the current. Even most traders who play off reversals wait until it's actually happening instead of trying to play off extreme peaks and valleys."

"So you consider yourself a reactive trader and not a predictive trader?"

"Well, when we take an entry before a signal is given, we're predicting it will be given later. When we trade a stock at $600 simply because we believe it will go to $700, we are predicting."

She nodded. "Yeah, the best way to discover a trader's motivation is to ask them WHY they entered a trade. If they say: 'I bought it because it can't go any lower,' or 'I bought it because I believe it will go to $100,' or 'I sold the stock short because it just can't go any higher,' then they are predicting not reacting. A reactive trader says things like: 'I bought it because it broke out over resistance of a 3 month price base to all-time highs,' or 'I shorted it because it broke down under long-term price support levels,' or 'I bought it because it bounced up off a key support level or it broke out over short-term resistance.'"

She took a dainty sip of her coffee.

"A reactive trader needs a reason to take a trade based off a price action that appears to give them a probability of success; a predictive trader needs only a belief or opinion to take a trade. A reactive trader trades based on external reasons and chart price action; a predictive trader trades based on internal reasons and beliefs. Reactive traders trade for specific reasons, letting the charts guide them in entries, exits, and position sizes."

"Yes," New Trader said. "A typical long entry for a trend trader would be based off of strength in the price move overcoming a key resistance area. If a stock goes from $100 to $200, it has to first go to $101, $102, $110, $150, etc.

If a growth stock is trading between an $80 support level to a $100 resistance level for three months and then after earnings closes at $103, all the sellers have been overcome below $103 and the odds are that it will go even higher. Before the breakout happens, there's no real reason to expect a stock will go higher than $100. Many stocks never break out and could fall back to $70 or $50. A trend trader is looking to buy a stock that is making higher highs and higher lows day after day. That is proof of a trend. A break above resistance proves it has gone higher and it is possible to keep going higher and can go higher still. For swing traders, a bounce off a support level is confirmation to buy if the bounce does not lose support and roll over. The reactive trader is looking for confirmation. A predictive trader is just guessing," New Trader said, his excitement palpable.

Jane nodded and smiled her eyes clear and bright as she continued his thoughts.

"A reactive trader will exit a losing trade when the price move proves they are wrong. A reactive trader also exits a winning trade when it stops moving in their favor, not at a target price. Say a stock moves from $103 to $200 and never falls back below a $5 trailing stop until it goes to $200 and reverses to $190. The trader didn't exit at a $125 price target or a $150 price target because he rode it all the way until it finally has a strong reversal back through a key support level at $190. Of course, these are principles that you need in trading. You need a better reason for an entry than a warm, fuzzy feeling and a nebulous belief."

He laughed.

"Yeah, your position sizing should also be a function of the volatility of the stock's price range. If you are trading a $100,000 account and want to risk no more than 1% in any one trade, or rather a $1,000 loss, then the recent trading range will help your position size. If your stock moves $10 a day on average, then you can only trade 100 shares of the stock and risk a $10 move against you. If it trades in a $5 daily range, then you can trade 200 shares and risk a $5 move against you. Of course, you may want to trade smaller and ensure that your entry is at a spot where a move against you in those dollar increments will not just be noise inside the trend you are trying to capture. The bottom line is that if you want to be a successful trader there must be a reason for everything you do, based on the facts of actual price action and on the charts."

She nodded. "Being a factual trader is much more profitable than being a fictional trader."

"Traders who start telling themselves stories and believing their own bull generally head down the road of capital destruction. There must be a quantifiable reason to take a trade. There must be real reasons for entries, exits, position sizing. Trading on a whim almost never works. Trading based on actual price action, on the other hand, has a great chance of working because you're flowing in the same direction as the markets. The markets don't care what we think or believe. They're like a train. We can either ride them or be run over."

Jane sighed. "I suppose this means I'll have to throw away my crystal ball..."

New Trader laughed. "I guess we both will... I didn't

know you were a trader."

She gave him a half smile. "Yes... a bit... I'm working at the cafe to bring up my capital. My goal is to be able to trade full time. I've been talking to Rich Trader too, a bit. He's an amazing help."

"I know, he's a veritable fountain of knowledge."

"You haven't been by for a while. Did something happen?"

He looked at her, not sure if he really wanted her to know or if she really even wanted to know, but he decided to go ahead and say it.

"I broke up with my girlfriend."

"Oh... I'm sorry."

He shrugged. "At least I didn't marry her."

She laughed. It wasn't the usual response he got, especially from women, but he found that he rather enjoyed it – as well as the company of another trader who wasn't quite so seasoned.

CHAPTER 8

A good trade is based on your own personal edge; a bad trade is based on your opinion.

"A trader should have no opinion. The stronger your opinion, the harder it is to get out of a losing position."

— *Paul Rotter*

"Do you know what one of the hardest things for new traders to wrap their mind around is?" Rich Trader asked when New Trader had finally settled in to a comfortable chair as he showed up to meet with him again.

"What's that?"

"That the best traders are very flexible in their opinions," the older man continued. "The vast majority of rich traders aren't trying to predict what will happen or how far a price move will go; they're trying to understand what's happening in the current market and what has happened historically. Rich traders try to merge their own trading with the chart and price actions, trying to move in sync with the market moves. They understand that the market doesn't care what their individual opinion is. You don't become a rich trader by forming an opinion but by seeing the pattern prices have formed and may form again based on the nature of the human psychology of greed and fear."

New Trader nodded.

"Because the market will go where it pleases and trends

will feed off themselves."

"Exactly, trying to trade against a trend with momentum is like trying to argue with a speeding train. The train will eventually run out of fuel and stop but it is unprofitable to bet against a moving train until you can identify it is actually slowing down and losing momentum. The key is that trades should be made based on facts, not personal opinions. The most dangerous thing a trader can do is develop a mental bias and let the bias affect the way they see price action and chart patterns. A stop loss and a trailing stop are powerful ways to follow actual price action and avoid opinions. Many great traders let stop losses and trailing stops do the heavy lifting for them."

"So a trader has to know why they entered a trade, what the signal was, and where the exit signal is."

"Yes... There are three main types of traders. The first are purely mechanical traders who have done their homework in back-testing historical price action, seeing what works and what doesn't. Mechanical traders do their discretionary work in building their trading model and then let the model run. They know 100% what they will do under different price action circumstances. Their discretionary work continues after the market closes for the day, when they question the continued validity of their system. Mechanical traders do a lot of homework before changing a mechanical system. They do not trade their opinions; they trade the validity of the opinions they back-tested that were historically robust in different market environments. The discretion happens in the research so that the trading can be mechanical in the live action of the markets," Rich Trader said, taking a sip of coffee before continuing.

"The next group is rule-based discretionary traders. While these traders believe that their own decision-making process gives them an edge, they still trade inside a framework of rules that keep them safe and profitable. Discretionary traders can decide if they want to take a signal or not and how many trades to put on at any one time along with position sizing. Most traders have rules about risk management, maximum risk exposure, draw downs, entry signals, exit parameters, and even rules about their trading psychology. The rules are based on many years of personally learning what works and what doesn't and are created as a safety net to avoid past mistakes. The trading rules aren't meant to keep traders from the freedom to trade; they are meant to keep traders safe from themselves."

"And I suppose the last is Mr. Know-it-all?" New Trader said.

Rich Trader nodded.

"That is the mindset of most new traders against the rocks of reality. Even some professional money managers trade their own opinions above any real research or trading education. The Know-it-all Traders' strategy is very simple. They buy what they 'like' and sell what 'has to go down.' They believe their intellect and gaming skills are far greater than the majority of traders and the market as a whole, even though they have no facts confirming this. They are loud and opinionated and believe deeply in their convictions of what price action will happen next. Their trading is little more than spur-of-the-moment decision-making based on their beliefs. These are the traders who think they are special and very clever; unfortunately, many times they start their trading careers in markets that are conducive to their styles. Many times they confuse bull markets with stock-picking skills and personal genius. They confuse huge monthly returns with being smart when really they are setting up for an eventual account blowup due to positions sizing and too much open risk, which gives them big returns but which also gives them big losses when the market dynamic changes. They confuse their feelings of superiority during long winning streaks with the mental strength to come back from draw downs in capital and losing streaks. The know-it-all-trader has no edge – just a lucky rabbit's foot and self-delusion. While this trader may be profitable for many years, eventually the markets take back every penny of the profits given away by luck, and lucky money is taken back much faster than it is given away. These lucky traders slowly climb the stairs of profitability but then fall down the elevator shaft as they quickly give back all profits and learn the dangers of leverage and position sizing as all profits are returned to the market and maybe even most of the original trading principle due to a lack of respect for extreme risk events."

"So which have you been?" New Trader asked.

Rich Trader chuckled. "Why, I've been all of them, of course. The better question is... which are *you?*"

"I suppose I'm still stuck in the know-it-all phase... I've let my opinions drift into my trading, and it's one of my biggest adversaries. I get into trouble when I start fighting a trend I should be following, or buying support levels when I should be waiting for a snap back rally with strength. My biggest problem is that I drift from my trading plan while the market is open and think I'm smarter than the trading plan I wrote while the market was closed – even though I have proven time and time again that I'm not. My opinions have been... expensive, to say the least. And it also seems that the stronger my opinion is, the more prone I am to trade too big, and that almost never ends well since I don't want to stop out and admit I'm wrong. Further, the bigger size of the trade, the more engaged my emotions are, which compel me to do foolish things that I would never do when trading smaller."

"The key to trading without opinions hurting trading performance is to trade using a systematic approach. You need to have quantifiable reasons for all entries and exits that are hard to get around if you follow your trading plan. Many traders find a mechanical approach easier to follow because it removes the discretionary, emotional trader entirely, which of course is the weakest link to any trading system. A discretionary trader needs to have entry rules that put them on the right side of the market: break outs, trading above a key moving average, focusing on higher highs or lower lows in their time frame, etc."

"Replacing my opinions with a systematic approach seems to be an edge in itself."

"Exactly, the ability to follow the price action without a personal bias is a very powerful edge that few traders ever get to or even understand. Always seek to ride the wave that is occurring now as best you can rather than sit back with opinions on how far the wave will go or when it will end and miss the ride altogether. In the markets money is made by trend capture in your time frame, not opining on what should be happening now."

New Trader nodded, glancing around the cafe.

He was strangely disappointed not to see Jane.

CHAPTER 9

A good trade is made using your own timeframe; a bad trade changes timeframe due to a loss.

"The key is consistency and discipline. Almost anybody can make up a list of rules that are 80 percent as good as what we taught our people. What they couldn't do is give them the confidence to stick to those rules even when things are going bad."

– Richard Dennis

"A good trade is based on predetermined parameters," Rich Trader began as they drank their favorite coffee in the quaint coffee shop New Trader had discovered not too long ago. It was nice and quiet, decorated in subtle blues with comfy chairs and quality beverages – a perfect place to meet and talk.

"That means the trader knew the position size they would trade before they entered. The trader had a quantified entry signal based on price action at the right level, and would the position be held until the stop loss was hit and taken, acknowledging that the trade was wrong. The stop loss would be triggered at a price level that showed the trader they were wrong and it was time to exit. The amount of money lost would be within the guidelines of total trading capital that could be risked and lost on one trade without putting the trader in the risk of ruin zone over the course of many trades. The trading vehicle that was traded was on a previous watch list and the trader had researched price action history to understand what did and did not work. That is the formula for a good trade. A bad trade is when the trader strays from quantifying a trade to following opinions, emotions, and ego. "

"So basically, a trade is a serious business transaction, based on the risk/reward ratio, probabilities, possibilities, and managed risk? You should know exactly what you're doing in every single move in every single trade?"

Rich Trader nodded.

"Creating the trading plan isn't usually the problem. The problems generally begin when the trader tries to stay disciplined while the market is open. Greed, fear, ego, and stress weren't there when the plans were created, but all show up and want to be heard when the market is open. A good trader is disciplined and able to follow a plan rather than emotions and opinions. That's hard enough, but when the market environment changes and a string of losses occur, that amplifies everything. The trader has to pre-plan how to handle draw downs in capital by trading smaller, by having fewer positions at one time, or by just not trading until there is a signal indicating that the market environment may be favorable again. Traders find out very quickly that they are the weakest link in any trading system the moment they go live and it's time to follow the predetermined plan."

"So most traders lose because they just can't stick to the original plan?"

Rich Trader took a sip of his hot coffee before replying with a sigh. "They may have a great trading system and just be in a bad market. Instead of getting through the market environment, they try to fit their system and style to the market they are in. That really starts messing them up when a trend follower tries to day trade or a swing trader tries to start selling options. It takes a lot of time and work to get an edge in any type of method and it is not easily transferred to trading on a different timeframe. If you want to trade multiple systems with different methods, that's fine, but each must be researched properly before they're needed. A major change in trading style based on the market environment should be preplanned, not a spur-of-the-moment adjustment because of a losing streak. Large samples of trades should be researched before considering adjustments to back-tested trading systems."

"I see. So you're saying plan, trade on paper before you trade with real capital. I need to make well thought-out decisions based on facts and not just based on losing money or losing control of my emotions. My decisions should grow out of research and planning rather than reacting to outcomes that may be random and temporary and just noise in the greater scheme of the next 100 trades."

"Style drift in trading usually doesn't work out, while researching and trading multiple methods is all right if you have put in the work to determine that they have robust back test history. Of course, risk exposure has to be determined with all open positions, as well as the level that the trading vehicles are correlated to determine total open risk exposure. I think Bruce Lee summed it up the best."

"Bruce Lee?"

Rich Trader chuckled. *"'Knowing is not enough; we must*

apply. Willing is not enough; we must do". Bruce Lee may not have been a trader, but he knew a thing or two about discipline."

"That's the real difficulty, leaping from theory to practice, from learning to doing, from principles to action. It's a lot like training for a sporting event with plenty of time for reflection and practice but then having to compete live with all the stress and strain of performance. It's a very different experience; the live event is the time to do or die. Results will be judged on success and failure yet emotions and stress show up that were not there during practice. There's an audience and there are expectations from the fans and the athlete."

"Yes," Rich Trader said. "What usually separates athletes at the highest professional level is their mental edge. All professional athletes are gifted physically, but the winner is usually the one who is able to function at the highest level at the most important time. Many traders have an audience such as a spouse, a family, or other traders who add to the pressure of success. At least, that has been my experience. Study and research had little to do with my live trading. My trading with actual large amounts of money seemed to be an exercise in my ability to be disciplined and manage stress."

New Trader sighed. "Yes, well, I don't have much of an audience right now, except you, of course."

"Well, don't let it bother you. It was probably for the best in any case. After all, target practice is a very different experience than a gun fight. The best traders come down to those who are able to manage stress the best, persevere, and keep their egos in check. The best chart readers and analysts are rarely the best traders. Trading is performing live on stage; analyzing is like being a judge on the sidelines. Judges are paid for showing up at work while performers on stage are paid for performance over the long term."

"I've learned that a top trader skill is the ability to do in real time what you had planned to do before the market opens. Following a trading plan seems simple until green and red numbers are flashing in front of your eyes and money is growing or evaporating. I've also learned that my real test as a trader comes after strings of losses and strings of wins. Losing streaks activates my ego to want to trade big and get back those losses quickly and my big wins and winning streaks decreases my fear of losses and makes me feel invincible and like a genius who has no need for risk management. I have to grow up and stop going down either of these paths and just focus on consistency. All this has been golden advice today. Thanks."

"Of course, anytime," Rich Trader said with a kind smile. "I always enjoy our little talks.

CHAPTER 10

A good trade is made in reaction to current price reality; a bad trade is made based on personal judgment.

"Pure price systems are close enough to the North Pole that any departure tends to bring you farther south."

— *William Eckhardt*

"Quantify, quantify, *quantify,* you must know where you'll be getting in and where you'll be getting out once you are in. You have to know your numbers; your entry price, your exit price, your positions size and what you'll be trading. No trade should be taking place in the real world until it's first planned out on paper. The price is your guide and your plans have to be based on the potential probabilities of different price action scenarios playing out," Rich Trader began. "It's your job as a trader to plan how you will react to different price action, patterns, and increases in volatility. Your plans can make you money because you're not trying to predict what will happen; you're adjusting in real time to what *is* happening. In essence, you are not trying to beat the market; instead you are trying to be the market. There is a big difference."

"So I have to have a laser-like focus on trading price, not emotions, not opinions, and certainly not my ego."

"Reactively trading price action as it unfolds versus trying to predict what will happen in the future is one of the biggest secrets of rich traders. Rich traders know that they don't have a crystal ball or time machine and they understand that they're not prophets. And it seems that many new traders, talking heads, and gurus skipped that day of trading school. While bad traders go in search of "market calls, "hot stock picks," "gurus," and "Holy Grail trading systems," rich traders are busy studying historical price action, price patterns, back testing trading systems, and studying chart action for clues as to what is actually happening in the present moment."

"I see... So rich traders are more like scientists than traders, and bad traders sound more like gamblers than traders. Rich traders try to scientifically figure out what works through experiments and confirming data, while bad traders look to pick up easy money lying on the street."

"I can tell you from personal experience there's no easy money in trading that will just jump into your pocket. I know now that all trading profits come from work, taking on risk, and managing positions in the right way," Rich Trader said. "You need to always be trading the facts about price action. Don't let your view of the price action be skewed by the open position you are holding. Always do what the price says to do inside the parameters of your system and timeframe. Take the entry, ride the trend, buy the bounce, trail the stop, take the loss. Price action needs to drive your trading bus. Your job is to make sure you are on the right bus."

"Money is made in the markets by going with the current flow. A profitable strategy is learning to identify the potential for a trend and then capturing that trend with the right entry; letting your winner run until you are stopped out as the price breaks near term support levels for the trend in your timeframe. Trend capture is best done by following price action, not having an opinion. A market can run farther than you expect and it can also fail to trend. A mechanical stop set at a price level indicating you are wrong can save you a lot of mental and financial capital. A stop that tells you to exit is a better plan than arguing with the market price action.

It is much better to let a bounce off the bottom of a low price level happen first, then take a position long after confirmation has happened instead of trying to predict when it has gone too low and is "due" for a bounce."

"So one key to trading price action is to wait for confirmation for an entry, instead of just anticipating what I think is going to happen."

"Yes, exactly, your odds of a successful trade are usually better by buying into strength and selling short into weakness. This way you're going with the flow of your timeframe. The next step is trailing the winner with a stop or taking a stop loss at the level that shows you are wrong. It's not about prediction; it's about reacting."

"A big mistake many traders make is trying to go short in a bull market because they think prices are too high. In a bull market, indexes and individual stocks tend to have support levels but not long term resistance bull market trends tend to keep making higher highs and higher lows. Easy money is made to the up side until the market rolls over to lose support and goes into a downtrend. While some really good day traders can scalp shorts intra-day, the majority of longer-term swing traders would do better to buy at support levels than try to sell resistance levels short. And of course, trend followers should stay long in the trend as it continues to hold up. Always trade in the direction of the longer-term trend of your time frame where the easiest money is located. Betting on a reversal of a longer-term trend is wrong more times than right," Rich Trader said.

"Running with the bulls in a bull market and riding with the bears in a down trend seems like it would be a better trading experience than trying to fight against the flow of price action," said New Trader.

Rich Trader nodded.

"Another consideration for traders who are trading price action is that markets go from low volatility to high volatility in cycles, with daily price range expansion, gaps, and sharp quick reversals in price action trends. Many trading systems fall apart in volatile markets, especially shorter-term trend trading systems which key off short-term moving averages. Others, like long option strangles and straddles, do very well if exited at the right time. There are even traders who sell options to get the bigger implied volatility premium that is priced in and profit when the volatility falls back to lower levels and is priced out of the options. Just as price trends, volatility, chart patterns, and trader psychology also trend in the markets. "

CHAPTER 11

A good trade is made after identifying and trading with the trend; a bad trade fights the trend.

"The answer to the question, 'What's the trend?' is the question, 'What's your timeframe?"

— Richard Weissman

"I know that trading following a trend is where the money is made and that is how I try to trade, but how do you identify the trend?" New Trader asked one sunny afternoon as he sat on Rich Trader's patio.

"Well, it depends. The first thing the trend depends on is your timeframe. A long-term trend following trader may be long based on the weekly or monthly chart, while a day trader may be short based on the intra-day 15 minute chart. Both make money in their position when they exit. The key is looking at the direction of the price in your timeframe. Examine and quantify support and resistance levels along with moving averages. Some traders also use Elliott Waves and Fibonacci price levels."

"There are many ways to measure the path of least resistance," Rich Trader said as he led the younger trader to his office and sat at his computer, pulling up daily charts from his favorite website.

- Moving averages are one way to quantify where the current price is in relation to an average of prices over a specific timeframe. If the current day's price is over the 5-day moving average, it could be said to be in an uptrend in that timeframe on the daily chart.

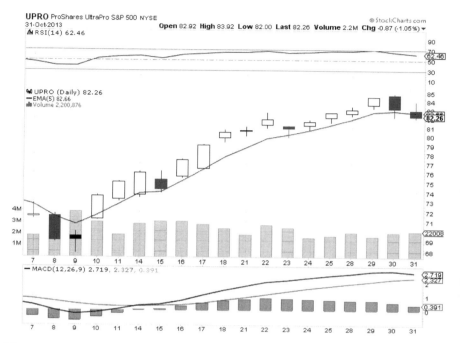

Chart courtesy of StockCharts.com

- With higher highs and higher lows over a time frame it could be said that the market is in an uptrend.

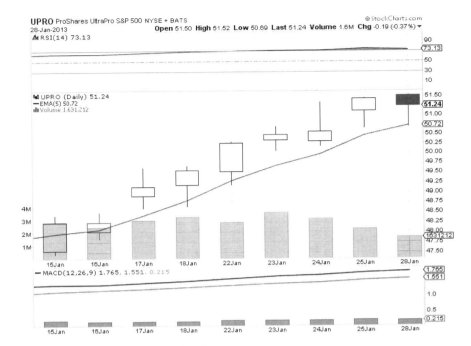

Chart courtesy of StockCharts.com

- Lower highs and lower lows are an indication of a down trend.

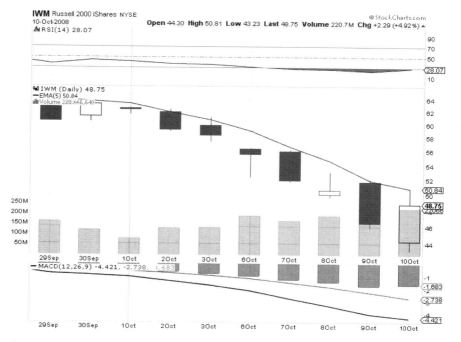

Chart courtesy of StockCharts.com

- A break out of a trading range with a new price above or below the established range of support and resistance can also be a signal and indicate a new trend emerging out of a price consolidation period. A break down out of a trading range that makes a new low means that buyers are no longer willing to pay the asking price of support and that sellers are willing to sell for less than support in that timeframe.

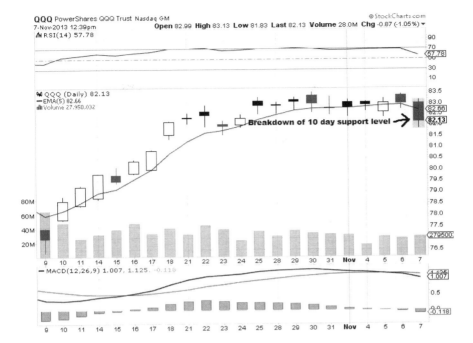

Chart courtesy of StockCharts.com

- In a break out over resistance sellers will no longer sell for less than resistance and buyers have to pay more than resistance to get in.

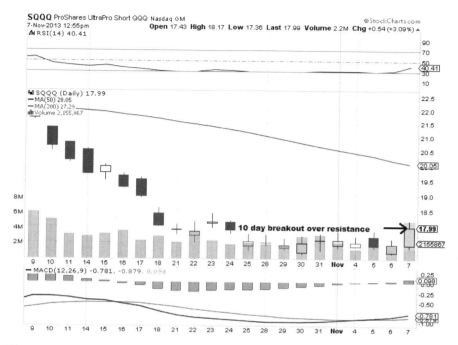

Chart courtesy of StockCharts.com

"A trend is best entered at the point where something quantifiably changes in price action, like new highs or new lows in a trader's timeframe. All-time highs and all-time lows is a favorite break out strategy for many trend traders. Really, all traders, regardless of their method, are trying to profit by understanding and betting on a trend," Rich Trader said, continuing his impromptu lecture.

- Buying all-time highs is trying to capture a breakout trend.

- Selling short all-time lows is trying to capture a break down trend.

- Buying a strong reversal off the bottom is an attempt to capture a rally back to resistance.

- Selling short a breakdown at resistance levels is trying to profit from a retracement to support.
- A trader who shorts over extended markets in either direction is trying to capture a trend where the market reverts back to its mean.
- Out-of-the-money option buyers are betting on a strong trend to their strike price.
- Option premium sellers are betting that the trend is already priced into the option they are selling and that it will not go farther than that.
- Day traders are trying to profitably capture daily trends.
- Intermediate term traders are after profitable trends on the daily chart.
- Long-term trend followers are looking for the big trends on weekly charts.

"Almost all traders are trend traders, whether they know it or not. The trader has to focus on quantifying how they will identify and capture trends in a profitable way on their timeframe," Rich Trader said as he turned to look at New Trader. "The entry should be at a high probability moment after confirmation that something has changed in the price action which may indicate a move in one direction. The entry level should have a good potential risk/reward where the trader is exposing 1% of trading capital at risk for the potential of making a 3% profit on total trading capital."

"So I really need to be focusing on price action to identify potential trends—not opinions, beliefs, or listening to others." "The success of your trading method will be determined by your ability to identify, enter, and exit trends."

"How do you best identify where an exit door is?"

"You'll want to be in the trend for as long as possible. You need the big wins to pay for your small losses. You look for warning signs in your trend trades that tell you the trend may be nearing its end. In fact..." Rich Trader continued, pulling out a piece of paper. "Here are the warning signs I look for as I trade trends off the daily chart."

- If an uptrend suddenly takes out a previous day's lows for the first time in many days, that could be a good place to take profits or be cautious.

- If a downtrend suddenly takes out a previous day's highs for the first time in many days, that could be a good place to take profits or be cautious.

- If the price violates a key short-term moving average that I am using and then price is going to close on the other side of that line for the first time since entry, I will exit there.

- An expansion in volatility and the average daily range will make me cautious if I am on the long side or make me lower position sizing if I am short.

- The loss of a support or resistance level for a recent gap in the chart is one exit signal.

- A huge gap and reversal against the direction of my trend trade would make me believe it is ending and I would exit.

"The key is that you must quantify what will make you enter and exit based on principles and chart study, not personal opinion; once you have that method planned out, follow it and adjust as you learn and grow as a trader."

New Trader nodded, looking over the list studiously.

"Yes... thank you for this."

Rich Trader just smiled. "Of course. How are you and Jane getting along?

New Trader flushed. "I don't know what you mean. I haven't seen her in days."

"Well, perhaps you should do something about that..."

New Trader scowled.

"I don't know why you keep trying to set us up..."

Rich Trader looked at him with sad, knowing eyes. "You seem lonely."

And there was nothing New Trader could say to refute that.

CHAPTER 12

A good trade is made using the trading vehicles you are an expert in; a bad trade is when you trade unfamiliar markets.

"My strategy works well because it's my strategy. I know the strengths and more importantly the weaknesses of what it is I do. It also works well because I allow it to work and stick with it even when it runs into difficult times. Nothing works well if you keep changing your approach. To be a master you must be a specialist, not a jack of all trades."

– Mark Minervini

"The reason I make money is because I am a top expert in the world for the markets I trade and the method I use. I've spent thousands and thousands of hours studying my market's price history, trends, charts, different trading environments, volatility, and seasonality. I win because I am in the minority that has done much more work than the majority. In the markets you will see that money flows from those who have not done their homework to those who have," Rich Trader said.

"So if I want to be profitable, I have to do more homework than my competition?"

"Of course. Just like in sports where the athlete who trains the hardest usually wins, it's the same for traders. Traders who prepare the most before they trade will likely be on the right side of the market. What most bystanders confuse for lucky performance by professional money managers and traders is usually the product of learning what the right method to trade is and then trading that way after doing much homework and back testing."

"I don't think I spent enough time in preparation for actual trading before I went live. I entered trading with superficial knowledge after a few books and a seminar, without really understanding the historical performance of many of my trading methods," New Trader said with a sigh. "I didn't really understand how different market environments completely changed the dynamics of how my method played out. I thought I was an expert on what I was trading and I entered trading with a mere pocket of knowledge and far too much hope. I should have had a truckload of knowledge and a bucket full of reality."

Rich Trader chuckled. It was an all too common mistake.

"You have to be so knowledgeable and so secure in your faith that you can trade your markets profitably that it will put your mind at ease. You can't just hope you know what you're doing; you have to know for a fact that what you're doing will work. You need quantifiable data that shows in print that your methodology works. You need to go through price charts line by line, using back testing tools, software programs, or forward testing a large sample size to show that what you are planning will work. You need a large enough sample size over enough data point and different market environments to prove to yourself that what you want to do will really work. You need this not only to save yourself the trouble of losing real money while you learn the hard way if your method works or not, but you also need to develop in yourself the faith and determination that it will work over the long term."

"I suppose so... After all, there's a huge difference between believing, hoping, and thinking what you're doing is going to work and actually *knowing* it will work. But if I'm a discretionary, rule-based trader, then I cannot quantify and test everything I do."

"No, everything in trading cannot be quantified and tested, but you can take large enough sample sizes of what happened in similar circumstances and get an idea of probabilities. If an index failed to break above a 75 RSI nineteen of the previous twenty times, it could be said that the odds are 1 in 20 or 5% that it will break above it this time. The odds may be even less that the upside risk is more, even if it does go higher. These kinds of principles can be embedded into a rule-based method."

"So an example for me would be that since an index like the S&P 500 is primarily a reversion to the mean type instrument, then once I can see through historical price action that the 75 RSI acts as resistance for advancing prices in the majority of circumstances, that is a great spot to initiate a short play as a reversion to the mean system trade?"

"Exactly. And those who have not studied that indicator will have no idea where the price ceiling is likely to be."

Chart courtesy of StockCharts.com

"I really need to narrow my watch list and master a few trading vehicles," New Trader muttered, thinking aloud.

"If you find the rhythm of a few things and understand their tendencies and price history, you can do very well. My money came from focusing on a few, not struggling with many."

"What do I need to be focusing on to learn about them?" New Trader asked.

- "Well, let's see..." Rich Trader said as he started naming them off.
- Typical patterns they trade in
- Current trading range

- Key moving averages that act as support and resistance
- Longer-term support and resistance
- How it acts historically after different types of news events
- Time of the month behavior
- Seasonality
- First day of the month behavior
- Does it tend to trend or revert to the mean?
- How does it usually act in relation to key technical indicators?
- What is its current daily average trading range?
- What is its current weekly average trading range?
- What is its current monthly average trading range?
- How liquid are the options?
- What is its history for volatility?

"And of course, the most important question: How will you use this information to create a profitable system?"

"Well, now that I know what work needs to be done, it's simply a matter of doing it. It's time to get out the old spreadsheets and get to work."

PART III

MANAGING RISK TO STAY IN THE GAME

"The key to long-term survival and prosperity has a lot to do with the money management techniques incorporated into the technical system"

— Ed Seykota

CHAPTER 13

A good trade risks only 1% of total trading capital; a bad trade does not have a set amount of risk.

"There is a random distribution between wins and losses for any given set of variables that define an edge. In other words, based on the past performance of your edge, you may know that out of the next 20 trades, 12 will be winners and 8 will be losers. What you don't know is the sequence of wins and losses or how much money the market is going to make available on the winning trades. This truth makes trading a probability or numbers game. When you really believe that trading is simply a probability game, concepts like 'right' and 'wrong' or 'win' and 'lose' no longer have the same significance. As a result, your expectations will be in harmony with the possibilities."

– Mark Douglas: 'Trading in the Zone'

When New Trader went to meet Rich Trader at the cafe, he saw Jane getting ready to leave, looking pale and a bit ill.

"Jane, are you all right?" he asked her with a slight frown.

"Oh... yes, I'm fine, thank you... I just made a crucial mistake, is all..." she said, muttering under her breath.

"What do you mean?"

She looked up at him, seemingly guilty.

"I didn't count how big my loss was going to be... I got so swept up with dollar signs in the high that I didn't see the risk or the chances of my being wrong."

"I see," New Trader said. "That must have been hard."

She laughed. "I felt like I was going to – well, you're about to eat so I won't describe the feeling. But honestly, if I spent half the time managing risk as I did with my silly get-rich quick scheme that I should *know* better than to use, I'd probably survive this learning curve better and be on my way to being a profitable trader."

New Trader smiled. "Don't worry. I'm sure you'll get through this. You have to stop focusing your time and energy on your entry and potential profits and put more effort into risk management. You aren't just looking at potential profits, right? You have a setup and entry signal?"

She rolled her eyes, some color returning to her face.

"Of course I do!"

"All right, so you're probably concerned about the perfect setup and taking your entry signal for a good chance at a profitable trade. Then after your entry, you're thinking about a target price and where to take future progress. Am I guessing about right?"

"Maybe," she said with a weary smile.

"Right. I did the same thing. It's actually the backwards way to do things if you want to survive in trading. The first thing you need to think about is how many losing trades in a row you can have and still survive with your account intact. That's crucial, because while investors hold assets that fluctuate in value, traders actively enter and exit trades and can lose over and over again, grinding down their account value and destroying their capital. It's especially crucial for traders who use options and futures to trade with extra leverage. If you trade too big and lose too many times, you can end up with nothing or even worse, owing the broker money if they were on margin or sold options or futures short.

"Oh, I see," she said. "So I'm trying to survive even before I try to profit?"

New Trader shrugged. "Pretty much. The potential for blowing up is pretty real for a trader who isn't respecting risk or the potential for blowing up their account. The risk of ruin is how likely you are to blow up your account capital. Most people consider a 50% drawdown to be ruined because then you need a 100% return to get back to even."

"What do you mean 100% to get back to even? Wouldn't it be 50% to get back to..." she paused, thinking a moment. "Well, no, that's right, isn't it? As your capital is lost, you have less to rebuild with, so compounding works against you on the way down. If you have $100,000 and you lose 50%, then you have $50,000 left, so if you have a 50% return you only have $75,000. You need to double it, as in a 100% return, to get back to even. If you lose 10% it takes 11% to get back to even, 20% and it takes 25% to get back to even... Goodness, a 75% drawdown would need a *300%* return!"

New Trader nodded. "Yes, that's why Rich Trader has always advised me to never have the draw down in the first place. It's a lot easier to grow capital if you don't have to deal with draw downs over 10%."

"Well, that certainly puts it in perspective... I need to just cool down my risky trading and my desire to win so badly that I try too hard."

"You can still have big wins; you just have to manage your position sizing, entries, and trailing stops. All I'm saying is to just not have any big losses. You should never lose more than 1%, max 2%, of trading capital on any one trade. It's just too hard to get your capital back if you run into a long losing streak when the markets get tough."

"Yeah, they're rough on the psyche too..." she grumbled.

"Rich Trader told me once that a trader risking more than 5% of their capital per trade is doomed to un-profitability in the long term. After five losses you're down 25%, after ten you're down to 50%. And there are very few traders, even if they have high winning percentages, that don't lose five to ten trades in a row per year. You have to be able to survive the duration of losses. Your probability of survival increase dramatically as you lower your percentage of capital at risk. So if you're risking 1%, your risk of ruin is almost 0 if you use it with a good trading system."

Jane nodded, "So if I'm wrong, I'm losing only 1% of my trading capital, and if I'm right I can make 2 or 3%... depending on *exactly* how right I am. The upside is left open, but the downside is capped. And my losses should all be about the same, with no outlying huge losses. The only outliers should be the big ones in the winning column."

"Yeah, you have to get your trading to a place where the losses won't kill you but the wins can make you a lot of money."

"Any advice for using the 1% max loss of total trading capital per trade rule?" she asked. "Well, let's see..." New Trader began. "You start with your trading account first, say you have $50,000. Now you should never lose more than $500 on any one trade if you're wrong. Your next step is to study the volatility of what you want to trade. If you are trading a stock that moves in a $5 average trading range each week, then you should likely only be trading 100 shares of this stock. If it is currently trading at $85 and it triggers an entry for you, then you can buy 100 shares and set your stop at $80 while you see based on the chart that it has the potential to be at $100 before it falls back under support to $80. You are in effect risking 1% of your total trading capital to make 3% of your total trading capital if the chart plays out."

"Right. So I figure out what I should risk in the trade first, then figure out my position sizing before I enter."

"Yeah, you'll be doing the opposite of the traders who don't make it in the markets. Risk will be your priority and this will enable you to keep the profits you make. Risk management is the Holy Grail of survival and long-term profitability in trading."

"Right. Well, thanks, New Trader. That was some really useful advice. Honestly, it's like I'm talking to a younger version of Rich Trader," she said with a laugh. "But I really do have to go now. I'll see you later."

"See you later," he said, watching her go, a warm feeling swelling up inside his chest as he made his way over to Rich Trader.

Comparing him to Rich Trader was probably the best compliment he'd ever received.

CHAPTER 14

A good trade risks $1 to make $3; a bad trade risks losing more than it plans on making in profits.

"At the end of the day, the most important thing is how good you are at risk control."

– Paul Tudor Jones

"Do you want to hear one of the most crucial aspects to trading success?" Rich Trader asked as they sat down for a meal.

"Of course."

"It's not very glamorous or exciting, but here's one of the keys to profitability versus losing money: Risk a little to make a lot. If you risk 1% of your trading capital, do it for the opportunity to make at least a 3% return on your capital. Risk $1 only for the opportunity to make $3. Only buy a stock at $100 with a $95 stop loss if it has the potential to run to $115. The reason successful option buyers make money even with a 50% winning percentage is because the wins are so big that they pay for the losses. Trend followers are profitable long term because they set themselves up for the really big wins."

Rich Trader took a sip of tea before continuing.

"The whole thought process behind the old Wall Street saying, 'Cut your losses short and let your winners run,' is that it creates a favorable asymmetry in your trading methodology. A 1:3 risk/reward ratio means that you are profitable with only a 33% winning percent and break even with a 25% winning percentage," he said, bringing out a napkin to write on.

Lose -$100

Lose -$100

Make +$300

After three trades your profit is +100 with a 33% winning percentage 1:3 Risk/Reward

Next Example:

Lose -$100

Lose -$100

Lose -$100

Make +$300

Break even with $0 with a 25% winning percentage 1:3 Risk/Reward (Before commissions and slippage).

Another example:

Lose -$100

Lose -$100

Make +$300

Make +$300

Profit $400 with a 50% winning percentage 1:3 Risk/Reward

"If a trader can get the right risk-versus-reward ratios in their trading system, they can have an edge that doesn't require a winning percent greater than 50% to be profitable. Having only small losses with big wins is an edge in itself and leads to profitability."

"I see," New Trader said. "Being right half the time with these sizes of losses versus wins is a very profitable risk management system. A very favorable risk/reward ratio creates robustness in your trading methodology from a money management perspective and eliminates the risk of ruin..."

"Yes," Rich Trader replied. "This frees the trader to focus on a great methodology that gives him key entries with a potential upside three times greater than the potential downside. Keeping the losses asymmetric versus the wins also alleviates a problem that most new traders experience: A few big losses giving back long-term profits quickly as a market environment changes, and what used to work stops working. While the risk/reward ratio is by no means a perfect science, it's a great blueprint to try to work inside of as a trading plan and method is built. Of course, the trader will have to deal with some price gaps in open positions that make losses bigger than planned and there will also hopefully be some really big wins that are even more than three times the losing trade during trends if profits are allowed to run with a trailing stop."

"It changes much of the dynamics of entries when you are looking to risk $1 to make $3 instead of risking a lot to make a little," New Trader said contemplatively. "It makes the trader consider the wisdom of selling option contracts even with high probabilities of wins because the losses during random outlier events can be devastating and wipe out long-term profits in one massive loss. Option buyers can be profitable if they trade small enough to survive the string of losses to get to the big winning trade which may be 10 to 20 times the size of the previous losses. Option buyers with a high winning percentage can be very profitable due to the built-in asymmetry in option contracts where they are constructed in a way that limits losses to the size of the contract, but have an unlimited upside as their delta expands."

Rich Trader nodded.

"Most trend-following systems work because they are trades on the side of the huge trends in plunging bear markets or parabolic bull markets. It's not magic; it is a favorable risk/reward ratio that is used while managing risk until they get the big payoff. A trend-following system is designed to find key points for entries which give good probabilities for a trend to begin. If the trend fails, they stop out for a small loss and try again for that big win. Many trend-following systems have very low winning percentages but at the same time huge winning trades which more than pay for all the losses given enough time. That is the real reason they are profitable," Rich Trader said, pausing as his tea is refilled.

"Regardless of whether a trader is trading a trend, swing trades, day trading, trading options, futures, Forex, or anything else, their profitability is based on only one thing: Their overall profits are bigger than their losses. That is the final judge of a trader. Can you risk a little to make a lot while surviving a string of losses? Risk management is really the final judge on whether we make it as traders or not, even if we have a great trading method and have the right mindset," Rich Trader said.

"This is really a shift in the way I should be looking at my trading," New Trader said thoughtfully. "A winning percentage of 50% should be accomplished even if entries were random. The weight is not on winning all the time but finding the big wins while capping the losses to keep them small. A few really big wins in a string of small losses will make a trader profitable. In building my trading system I should be looking for trades with a limited downside and potential to trend up from my entry. I will be looking at the probabilities of my trade being a winner that is three times the size of my stop loss level. This shifts my focus from winning trade percentage to trend identification and capture."

"All of trading is really a bet on identifying a trend in a certain timeframe, but *profits* come from making more money than you lose," Rich Trader said.

CHAPTER 15

A good trade follows a trading plan even during draw downs in account equity; a bad trade is a big trade made to quickly get even after a string of losses.

"Trying to trade during a losing streak is emotionally devastating. Trying to play "catch up" is lethal."

– Ed Seykota

"Do you know what the most dangerous moment for any trader is?" Rich Trader asked.

"What's that?"

"When they are down over 10% in their trading capital and want it back immediately. Draw downs lead to emotional and mental pain and the ego wants to prove that it is a great trader by getting the lost capital back as quickly as possible. This emotional urgency to get back losses quickly can set off a chain of errors for the new trader and maybe even more experienced traders," Rich Trader began. "Under the internal pressure to be made whole and relieve the mental pain of losses, traders will leave their trading plans so they are free to get their accounts back to even quickly without the bothers of risk management and proper position sizing. Some traders believe their decision-making process and opinion are better than the trading plan that took their capital down 10%. Then the fever strikes: They just need that one really big trade to take them back to even. So they increase their position sizing during a losing streak. They push down hard on the accelerator when they are driving in the wrong direction at a time when they should be tapping the brake to slow down."

"I can see how that could happen," New Trader said. "But when you're in a losing streak, that's the last thing you want to do, right?"

"Exactly, generally, if you have built a solid trading plan around a robust system with the right position sizing, then draw downs are more of a function of the markets simply not being conducive to your trading method. It is time to trade smaller and be patient until the market dynamics return to your type of trading. Trading big position sizes always leads to big losses; it is just a matter of time whether it is now or later. The way out of a draw down is to stick to your plan and survive it, not try to be a hero and get out of it in a few big trades."

"Yes, that's one of my biggest weaknesses. It's like I turn into a different person after I start losing money trade after trade. It's usually when the market suddenly changes dynamics from trending to chopping or range bound to trending. Suddenly my best trade setups quit working. Buying dips that don't hold, buying breakouts that don't follow through, or the volatility spike makes it necessary to trade smaller. When I have many losing trades in a row, my emotions and ego are activated, creating noise that lays dormant during winning streaks."

"Yes, but you can't listen to those small voices. You have to believe in your trading plan and methodology more than those whining voices in your head! This is the major line that separates rich traders from new traders: the ability to follow a plan and ignore emotions and ego," Rich Trader said, his voice taking an unusually stern tone. "The way you handle losses and losing streaks determines your success as a trader more than any other thing. Even winning trading systems don't work if you cannot handle losses correctly. Traders cannot be successful unless they can manage their emotions along with their money. Most traders lose when they abandon their discipline for whatever reason and trade freestyle. Survival as a trader is based on the ability to stay disciplined with entries, exits, and risk management. Once discipline is abandoned, the clock starts ticking to eventual ruin."

"Yes, you're right," New Trader replied. "That really hits home. I need to work on my skills of being bored without the need to do anything, the patience to trade only when the setup is there, and the ability to find something to do when I can't trade due to market conditions. A lot of the mistakes I make during draw downs stem from my desire to do some kind of work to get my money back. Not doing anything and just going to see a movie or read a book seems counter to the work ethic I've been raised with."

"Well, we make our money in trading not by simply doing something but by doing the right things – and sometimes the right thing is doing nothing. Trend traders have to leave winning trades to run. They have to leave choppy markets to chop. The way out of a draw down is simply to trade smaller and smaller until you start winning again and then trade bigger back to a normal size as the markets give entry signals that work," Rich Trader said. "It's crucial as you enter a losing streak to not be ruined financially, emotionally, or mentally. When you are down with multiple losing trades in a row, it is time to cut your position sizing in half and stop the bleeding, not increase it. If the losses continue, get down to trading a quarter of your normal size. It is crucial to lose the least amount possible in a losing streak and win the most possible during a winning streak. You do not want to compound a losing streak by trading bigger or miss an opportunity in a winning streak to maximize big wins."

"So I have to replace my urge to get back to even quickly with a desire to keep the draw down as small as possible. I need to see the possible trap and stop trying to get the cheese," New Trader said.

"When traders can see the dangers first instead of the potential money to be made, they have moved to a new level in their trading. When your account is underwater, that is the most dangerous time because you feel you must get back to the surface quickly. You start to drown in self-doubt and criticism about whether you are a good trader or your method works. You have to have enough faith in yourself and your system to stay the course, allow as little damage as possible to your account, and patiently take your trades until the winning begins again. Traders cannot base their decisions on their feelings or opinions during a losing streak; they must trade the facts and the plan regardless of circumstances. If there are tweaks to be made due to flaws in the plan, those should be done logically based on facts away from live trading and market hours, not based on emotional reactions to money lost or a draw down from a certain market environment."

New Trader nodded thoughtfully.

"So when I start to feel like I am drowning I should stay calm and focus on swimming, not panic and start flailing about. The way out of a losing streak is to keep trading positions as small as possible and then get on a winning streak. That is made difficult if I turn a losing streak into a bigger losing streak with big emotional trades."

"Exactly… The biggest danger in losing streaks and draw downs is when traders blow themselves up emotionally and mentally and turn a losing streak into financial ruin with a few really bad trades fueled by desperation. Traders can come back from losses of capital but they can't come back from a complete loss of confidence in themselves to make the right decisions under pressure."

"I think I understand."

CHAPTER 16

A good trade has a limited downside but an unlimited upside; a bad trade has unlimited risk and a limited profit.

"What's really critical is that you understand that you make money by cutting losses short and letting profits run. This will give you a positive expectancy system."

— Van Tharp

"You know what?" New Trader said as he pushed his meal around with his fork. "I think the closest a trader can get to the Holy Grail of trading is to have very small losses and very large wins in their trading system. After all, a trader can be profitable even with a very low win percentage if their wins are big enough. On the flip side, even a very high winning percentage system can be unprofitable if the losses are big enough. A high winning percentage winning system can even lead to the ruin of a trader's account if their stop losses and proper position sizing is not used to control and manage losses. The problem, I suppose, is how to keep your losses as small as possible..."

"Well, when you get into a trade, you have to know exactly where you are going to get out of it if you're wrong. The stop loss and exit has to be set just outside the normal price action. A stop could be set at a close below a key support, or a few percentage points below a key moving average," Rich Trader said, taking a sip of coffee.

"The biggest losses generally come from either being so confident in a trade that the trader has no exit plan or not taking your initial stop loss plan but instead holding and hoping that it comes back. These are formulas for really big losses. If you add in improper position sizing and trade too big at the same time, you are walking the tightrope with no net and the losses can be staggeringly huge. This is the formula for unprofitable trading."

New Trader nodded.

"Another way to control losses is to only put as much capital in a trade that you are willing to lose. A stock trader may put only 10% of their total trading capital into one stock position and an option trader may buy an option contract using 1% or 2% of their trading capital and risk it all since it has a capped possible loss but a theoretically unlimited upside potential."

"That makes sense... so what about techniques for having huge wins?"

"Well, for a big winning trade you have to have a great entry, either off a key support level to give a margin of safety or a break out above a defined price range. There are also chart patterns like cup with handles, flags, pennants, wedges, and others that can give you key high probability entries with the potential for a trend to emerge in your timeframe," Rich Trader said, pausing to thank Jane for refilling his coffee.

"After the right entry you have to set your stop loss at a level that proves you are wrong, not one that will take you out of the trade on mere noise inside a normal price range for your time frame. Stop losses have to be wide enough to allow you to stay in the trade and not be shaken out with stops, but be tight enough to keep your losses small and contained if the entry does not work. Traders must position size so that it will be hard to be shaken out of a good trade with a little noise and movement against them.

After you're positioned correctly you have to let the trade run as far as it will go. One way to do this is to use a trailing stop instead of a price target. A short-term moving average as a stop or a percentage trailing stop will keep you in a trade until it reverses all the way back and through your moving stop loss. So you will be in a trend for as far as it will go without predicting, guessing, getting out at a target price too early and missing a huge trend. The reason many trend traders and trend followers are so profitable is that they have trading plans that open them up to truly outlying huge moves in commodities, indexes, and growth stocks. Some markets provide moves that can change a trader's life or at least their account size permanently if they are on the right side of the parabolic moves. The key is to let the appearance of the end of the trend appear on the chart and in the price action without judging or anticipating it and taking profits prematurely, lock in profits at the end of the trend when it really bends."

"That sounds like trend trading."

"Well, while trend trader and trend follower trading methods by their very nature are designed to do this systematically, all traders can benefit from cutting losers short and letting winners run as far as they will go. If a swing trader enters at a key support level and it is lost then breaks to the down side and starts a downtrend, they still need to cut their losses. At the other end of the chart, if a swing trader has their trade travel all the way from support to resistance and it breaks out, they can still trail their stops and let it run."

New Trader looked up, smiling at Jane as she took away his plate.

"Also..." Rich Trader continued. "Option traders who trade from the long side have built-in asymmetry for their trading because they can only lose the capital it costs to hold the option contract, but they have built-in leverage and an uncapped upside profit potential if they let a winning option trade keep growing in a trend. Many types of traders can benefit from small losses and big winners, not just trend traders."

"So where do you go looking for these big potential trends?"

"The primary driver of trends is fear and greed. Traders' desire to make money or not to lose money is the cause of the majority of truly strong trends which create higher highs or lower lows for a longer period of time. Most years there are themes in each market cycle; there are different bull markets and bear markets going on all the time. They could be in gold, oil, a currency, equities as a whole, or a single growth stock that is believed to be changing the world."

New Trader nodded thoughtfully.

"I look for a strong trend emerging out of a very long-term price base. Gold could be in its own bull market and trend higher because the common belief is that the fiat currencies are doomed due to central banks printing too much money. The belief in peak oil and possible shortages looming could send oil to $150 a barrel during a parabolic uptrend. A growth stock can double or triple or even more in a very short period of time when the market believes that its product, technology, or business model will completely change the world and could have the growth potential to take over a sector or industry. My job is to find that fear and greed and trade that chart based on its price action for huge wins by participating in the trend and keeping my losses small."

"That's trend following, but what other trading techniques do you recommend?"

"The principles I have been explaining to you in our conversations work in all timeframes and almost all methods. If you are going to be a day trader or a swing trader, I believe it is crucial that you limit your watch list to just a few things to trade and become an expert and master of your trading vehicles. If you have done your homework and price research and have been trading one thing for many years that in itself gives you a nice edge over others because you know exactly the personality and character of what you are trading and how it tends to act at key levels and based on different popular indicators.

Remember though that profitable trading simply comes down to all your winning trades being bigger than all your losing trades. That is a key area to focus on above all else because that determines whether you are profitable or not regardless of your other statistics for your trading method. Big wins and small losses will make all the difference on your trading journey and determine if you make money trading or just keep paying tuition to other traders through your losses. All traders are trying to quantify and capture a trend in their own time frame while managing risk, their own emotions and ego. That is the core of all trading."

"Right," New Trader said with a quiet laugh, looking for their waitress.

He'd decided to take a risk in his personal life that day. He was going to ask her out.

CHAPTER 17

A good trade has an optimum position size for that trade setup; a bad trade is based on feelings, financial need, or confidence in a trade.

"I've talked to many folks who have blown up their accounts. I don't think I've heard one person say that he or she took small loss after small loss until the account went down to zero. Without fail, the story of the blown-up account involved inappropriately large position sizes or huge price moves, and sometimes a combination of the two."

– D. R. Barton, Jr.

It was a windy, rainy Wednesday when New Trader went to visit Rich Trader. This time he even had an umbrella.

They settled in front of the TV, paying no attention to the newscast.

"When the probabilities of your trade being right are best, you should trade your full position size at that time. It is a great advantage to understand the basic probabilities of different trade setups in different market environments. A gap up for a hot growth stock after earnings has a different success rate than a break out to all-time highs out of a price base for the third time in a month. Buying a third bounce off support of an index has a different chance of working than a break to new all-time highs out of a base for the same index. Different chart patterns and different trading vehicles have their own personalities and it is crucial that a trader does enough homework to understand those dynamics. What you want to do is have the biggest trade sizes when right and the smallest trade sizes when wrong. That comes from knowing the basic odds of each entry point working or not," Rich Trader said.

"So it's the different quality of setups? A trader needs different position sizing based on odds?"

"Yes, exactly. One example of this for me is that my trades on the short side are much smaller than my long trades. Going short the stock market is really trading against the historical long-term flow of capital and the down trends tend to be much more short-term and broken up by rallies even in bear markets overall. The long-side trends tend to be much smoother with less whip saw reversals because I am simply trading with the flow of capital."

"So what's an example of a very high probability trade for you?"

"One of my favorite trades is for a growth stock to break out of a one-month price base range to new all-time highs leading up into earnings. Another is a gap up after earnings for a growth stock. Of course with these types of trades I need the company of the stock to be unique and change the world in some way to create momentum from buyers piling into the stock. Of course, when I say full position I still mean to never risk more than 1% of trading capital through proper position sizing based on volatility and your accounts trading size," Rich Trader said, glancing at the door.

He seemed to be expecting someone.

"There is a very big difference between wanting to trade maximum position sizing allowed because of a high probability setup and getting greedy and risking a blow up of your account. Knowing the difference is crucial for long term survival as a trader. Most new traders do not understand the mathematical probabilities of the risk of ruin. The risk of ruin can be determined based on their capital risked per trade and winning percentage. No matter how sure you are of a winning trade, never expose your trading account to a position size that would put it at risk of ruin. A maximum position size may be risking 1% of total trading capital while a normal trade is risking 0.75% and taking ordinary trades may risk half a percent. Of course, the parameters you set are personal choices on your own personal trading plan."

"I have seen that. So much of what you have been trying to teach me is simply pointing me in the right direction, not giving me a system or method."

"Trading is a very personal undertaking, like many other things in life. If you went a matchmaker to learn the best way to get a spouse and have a happy marriage, the counselor would not give you their own wife. Instead, he would teach you the big universal principles that work in dating, in having a fiancée, and how to have a happy marriage so that you can go find your own wife. The specifics he uses for his own life and how he found a wife may not fit yours because you are a different person and your potential wife will be different."

New Trader's brow rose at that. It was an unusual comparison, but accurate.

"In relationships there are universal principles like listening, communication, respect, and romance, and the same applies to trading. The universal principles of trading are risk management, psychology, and a robust methodology. The difference lies in the specifics of both endeavors. One person's wife may like red roses while the other prefers dark chocolate. This does not mean one of these is bad. They are just opinions and both wives can be happy and both husbands can be successful," Rich Trader said.

"What if all winning traders are using the same principles but think they are all different because of different methodologies?"

"Yes, that is very true on many levels. Traders who agree on trader psychology, risk management, risk/reward, and even trend can get into heated debates with a religious fervor about why their specific methodology is best and point out the flaws in others. If a trader is ignorant of another trader's method it can get heated quickly through disrespect and judging."

"Isn't that the truth," New Trader muttered, thinking of his own little blog that had spun out-of-control conversations.

That was when the door opened and New Trader's expression became one of confusion.

"Jane?"

She looked up at him, smiled, and waved. "Oh, hi there, I just came by to drop off some things for my Dad."

"Your..." New Trader said, looking at Rich Trader incredulously. *"Dad?"*

Rich Trader grinned. "Of course. And honestly Jane, can't you even afford an umbrella?"

ABOUT STEVE:

Steve Burns has been an active and successful in the stock market since the late nineties. He is the author of six books published by **BN Publishing** (available at all major Internet retailers). Steve consistently ranks in the top 500 of all reviewers on Amazon.com; he is also one of the site's top reviewers for books on trading. He has been featured as a top Darvas System trader on DarvasTraderPro.com. He is a frequent contributor to TraderPlanet.com, Traders' Online Magazine, and SeeitMarket.com. His reviews of trading books have been featured on BusinessInsider.com. Steve's NewTraderU.com blog is frequently featured in the news at Forexfactory.com and on TheKirkReport.com. The author has been interviewed for the online version of The Wall Street Journal. He lives in Nashville, TN with his wife, Marianne, and they have five children: Nicole, Michael, Janna, Kelli, and Joseph, and one granddaughter, Alyssa.

ABOUT JANNA:

Janna is an avid reader and writer of fiction. She has read hundreds of books on the art of fiction writing and is a huge fan of fantasy fiction novels. She was the co-author of the top selling book "New Trader, Rich Trader," applying her skills to character development and plot.

CONTACT STEVE:

E-Mail: stephenburns@bellsouth.net

Twitter:@SJosephBurns

He blogs at www.NewTraderU.com

He created a Facebook page for New Trader U: https://www.facebook.com/NewTraderU

Steve runs the Facebook traders group: New Traders, Rich Traders, and Good Traders.

You can request to join through his personal Facebook page: https://www.facebook.com/SteveJBurns

REFERENCE SOURCES

http://www.tischendorf.com/quotes/

http://www.businessinsider.com/the-tk-best-things-paul-tudor-jones-has-ever-said-2011-8?op=1

https://www.facebook.com/theeconomicrevolution/posts/200709843379330

http://www.vantharp.com/tharp-concepts/position-sizing.asp

RECOMMENDED READINGS

You Can Still Make It In The Market by Nicolas Darvas

The Richest Man in Babylon - Illustrated by George S. Clason

Invest like a Billionaire: If you are not watching the best investor in the world, who are you watching?

New Trader, Rich Trader: How to Make Money in the Stock Market by Steve Burns

How I Made $2,000,000 in the Stock Market: Now Revised & Updated for the 21st Century

By Nicolas Darvas, Steve Burns

Stock Options: The Greatest Wealth Building Tool Ever Invented

By Daniel Mollat

Show Me Your Options! The Guide to Complete Confidence for Every Stock and Options Trader Seeking Consistent, Predictable Returns

By Steve Burns, Christopher Ebert

How I Made Money Using the Nicolas Darvas System, Which Made Him $2,000,000 in the Stock Market

By Steve Burns

TRADING SMART: 92 Tools, Methods, Helpful Hints and High Probability Trading Strategies to Help You Succeed at Forex, Futures, Commodities and Stock Market Trading

By Jim Wyckoff

How to Get Followers on Twitter: 100 ways to find and keep followers who want to hear what you have to say.

By Steve Burns

Available at www.bnpublishing.com